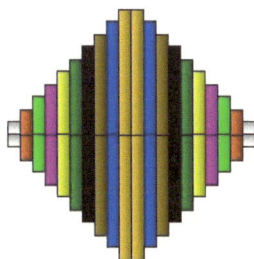

The Amazing Colour Factor Multiplication Square

1	2	3	4	5	6	7	8	9	10
2	4	6	8	10	12	14	16	18	20
3	6	9	12	15	18	21	24	27	30
4	8	12	16	20	24	28	32	36	40
5	10	15	20	25	30	35	40	45	50
6	12	18	24	30	36	42	48	54	60
7	14	21	28	35	42	49	56	63	70
8	16	24	32	40	48	56	64	72	80
9	18	27	36	45	54	63	72	81	90
10	20	30	40	50	60	70	80	90	100

A **Child's Play Maths** Resource.

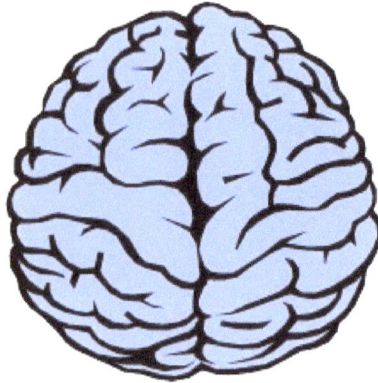

Your Child
Whole Brain Learning
and the
Amazing Colour Factor Multiplication Square

WHAT IS WHOLE BRAIN LEARNING?

Quite simply, whole brain learning occurs when as many of the brain's natural abilities as possible are utilized in any given learning situation.

It is sometimes referred to as 'accelerated learning' because accessing the brain's natural abilities inevitably speeds-up the learning process.

Using Cuisenaire rods together with the Amazing Colour Factor Multiplication Square brings many of the brain's abilities into play.

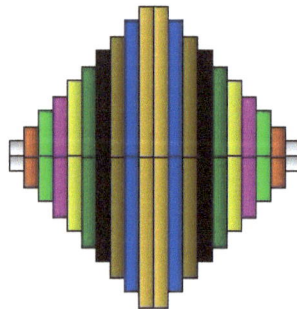

WHAT ABILITIES WILL MY CHILD USE?

Colour

Research undertaken by Backman, et.al and Allen reveal that colour is a greater stimulus for memory than verbal cues or objects.
Colour could and should play a far more significant role in the learning process within our schools.

Colour is a universal language.
Anyone who has travelled on the London Underground will appreciate the power of colour to help us find the way.

Colour will allow your child to become more adept at using the multiplication square in a variety of innovative ways.

Colour has a positive emotive impact upon the learner.
Red is engaging, yellow, beige or off white stimulate positive feelings while light blue and light green are said to be calming.
Weiner says that dark colours lower stress and increase feelings of peacefulness while red, orange and yellow spark energy and creativity.
Colour can help create the optimum learning environment.

Imagination.

Albert Einstein first became interested in the Theory of Relativity following a day-dream in which he imagined himself travelling on a beam of sunlight.
Daydreaming is one of the brain's most potent abilities.

The Big Picture

In his book '**The Learning Brain**', Eric Jenson states that 75% of teachers are sequential, analytical presenters. Unfortunately 70% of their students do not learn that way! He suggests that a better approach would be to start with a more global overview – The Big Picture – and then move to a more sequential approach.

A commonly held view when teaching children especially those considered to be 'slow-learners' is to feed them information a scrap at a time because that is all they are able to digest in one go. The fact is the more data we provide the brain the better, as what it loves to do is detect patterns and relationships.

When using 'The Amazing Colour Factor Multiplication Square' begin by giving your child the 'Big Picture'.

A suggestion on how to do this is offered later.
Please feel free to find your own way.

Imaging

Research reveals that 90% of all information that comes to our brain is visual.
Treisman and Gormican found that what the brain was designed to see soonest and easiest included colour and size. These are the basic properties of the rods and will help your child visualize the concepts necessary to ensure understanding.

Manual Dexterity

Thanks to the work of Dr Jean Houston we now know that stimulation of the body can stimulate the brain. Constant manipulation of the fingers has a positive impact on the mind. Play with the rods provides this kind of stimulation. Many experts now agree that stimulation at an early age is critical to the development of the child. In fact early-learning programs may well be essential for bringing up healthy children.

Our early years math program 'Child's Play Maths', is based on the natural development of children's learning via play and games using Cuisenaire rods. It embodies the principles discussed and is designed to be fun to use. It will ensure your child has a head start in mathematical development and an early introduction to whole-brain-learning techniques.

For more information please visit our web-site:
www.HelpYourChildSucceed.com

The Big Picture

From the outset explain to your child everything you are going to learn together.
Try setting it out as a mind-map.
Use colour to help find your way round the map

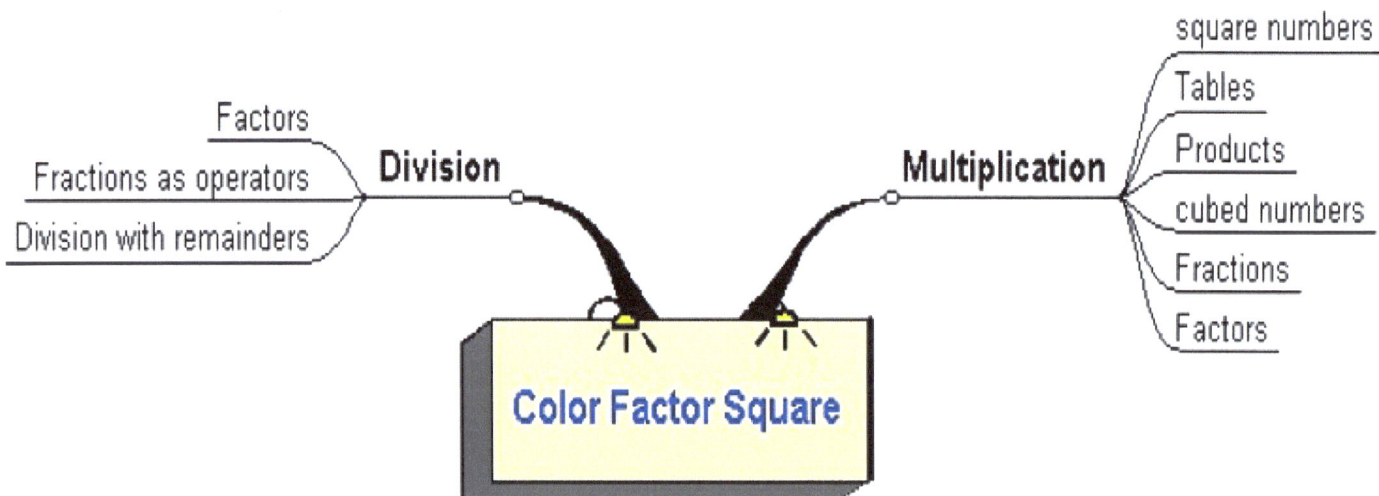

Factors

Fractions as operators

Division with remainders

Division

Color Factor Square

Multiplication

square numbers

Tables

Products

cubed numbers

Fractions

Factors

When 'mapping' use colour and diagrams to aid recall.
Create your own .
It will be far more effective because it is yours.

"If you don't know where you are going, you might wind up someplace else."

YOGI BERRA (B.1925)
American Baseball Player.

The Amazing Colour Factor Multiplication Square

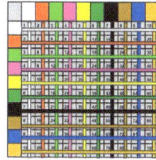

Colour

Colour is a great aid in helping children find their way around.
Ask:

"Where do the yellow lines and the blue lines meet?"

or

"What is '5 times 9?"

Repeat this exercise until you are sure children can find their way around the square without hesitation.

If they have been introduced to math via our early years program then, for the most part, they will learn to associate a particular number with a particular rod.

For example, yellow is 5 and Blue is 9.

(In '**Child's Play Maths**' we discuss why it is important children understand a rod can represent any value we choose to give it – the ability to 'abstract' - although for most of the time the value of white will represent 1).

Later we will see how colour can help children understand:

i) Cardinal Number.

ii) The Commutative Property of Multiplication.

For now we want to make sure children can find their way round quickly.

The Amazing Colour Factor Multiplication Square

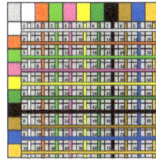

Imagination

The most effective learning takes place when:

i) The challenge is high and stress levels are low;

ii) Children are so motivated and absorbed by what they are doing they enter the flow state – time does not seem to exist and they are not conscious of those around them. This usually occurs when they are playing games machines!

iii) The whole of the learner is engaged in the learning process. It is a sensory and emotive experience.

This is when the imagination can be a very powerful tool.

Take another look at the 'Colour Factor Multiplication Square!'.

What might the coloured lines be? Railway tracks?

Bridges or tunnels?

A vast network of burrows?

A race circuit?

Imagination is a powerful ability in helping children remember and understand.

What's more, it's fun.
Involve your children in the game of imagining what the square could be.
I'm sure they will come up with plenty of suggestions that engage their particular interest.

A novel or unusual experience is always memorable and you will learn more about them as individuals in the process.

> "The Possible's slow fuse is lit by the imagination."
>
> **EMILY DICKINSON (1823-1886)**
> **American poet**

The Amazing Colour Factor Multiplication Square

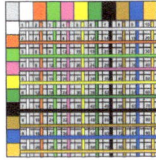

👁 Imaging

Being able to visualize the rods mentally will enable children to understand the underlying patterns and relationships that exist below the 'number surface.

Many children never grasp the concept of 'Cardinal Number'.

They have been taught only to see numbers as part of a counting process.

i.e.

☐ + ☐ + ☐ + ☐ = 4

Instead, if they can visualize the number mentally as a complete whole this speeds up the learning process.

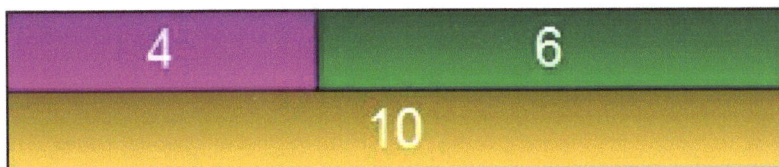

4 + 6 = 10

This helps them learn 'number bonds' very quickly.

It will also help them understand the commutative property of multiplication.

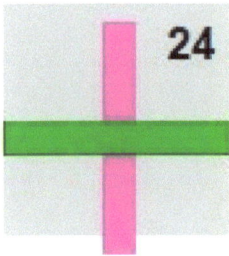

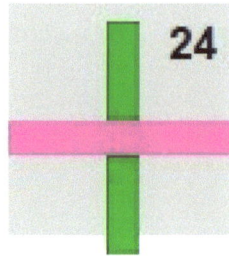

These squares might look similar and have the
same product but they are not the same.
They represent these patterns:

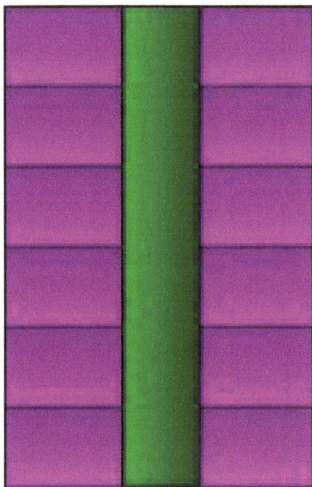

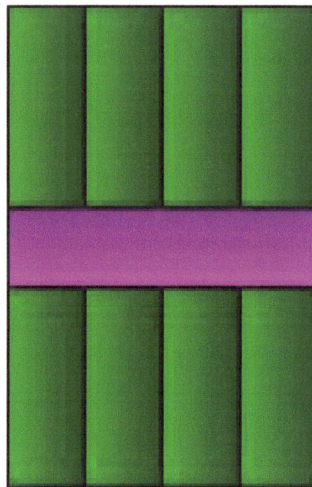

6 x 4 = 4 x 6 but they are obviously different.
Once children grasp this fact they immediately halve the
number of 'table facts' they have to learn.
The same holds true for number bonds because:
2 + 8 = 8 + 2

"... I never think in words: I
think in pictures."

Thomas Alva Edison

The Amazing Colour Factor Multiplication Square

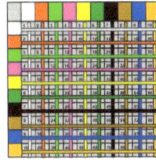

A Suggested Approach

1. Sequence of Tables

Tables can be introduced in a specific order to help children focus upon the commutative property of multiplication.

e.g.

2, 4, 8   3, 6, 9   5, 10

2. Crosses/Products

Task:

"Make a train of rods of only one colour."

e.g.

"Make another train, again using only one colour. Make it the same length as the first train."

e.g.

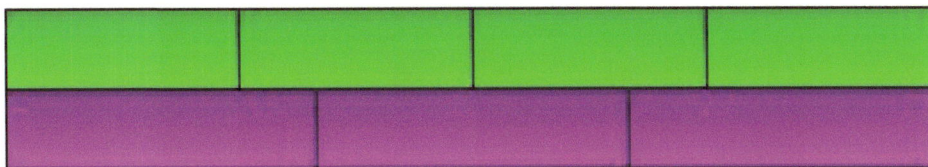

"Measure the length of the train using the orange rod (10)"

e.g.

"Now make a light green rectangle using the rods from the train. Make a pink rectangle using the rods from the train."

e.g.

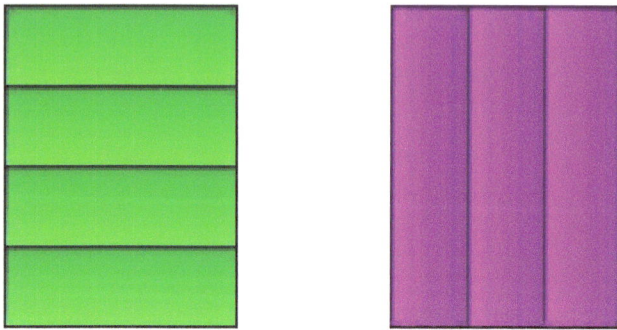

"*Will one rectangle cover the others?*"
The child physically covers one rectangle with the other.

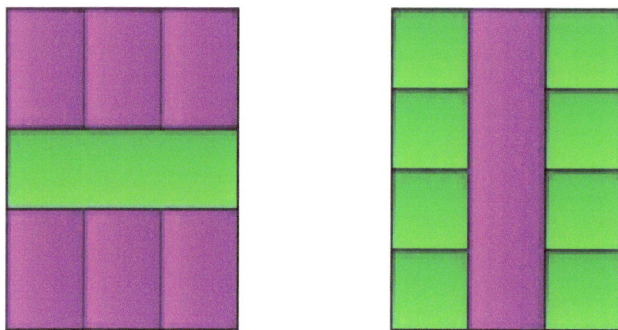

We can now show these rectangles by using a cross.
The rectangles represent the product.

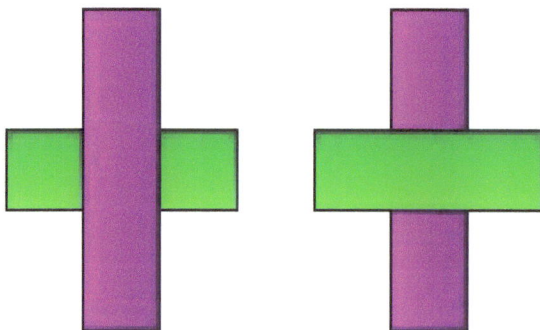

Once again the reverse crosses emphasize the commutative property of multiplication.

4 x 3 = 3 x 4

Repeat the exercise with different 'trains' until the child has grasped the concept.

To reinforce the concept choose a cross from the multiplication square and ask him/her to make the corresponding rectangle. e.g.

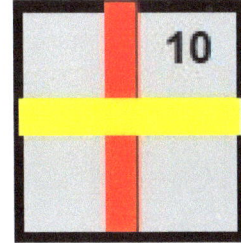

Can they find the 'reverse' crosses on the multiplication square?
Children will now begin to 'see' numbers as 'wholes'.
They will possess the ability to visualize 3 x 4 and 4 x 3.
Repeat similar exercises until you are sure children have fully grasped the concept.

Choose some crosses made of one colour.

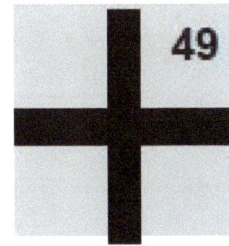

"Make the rectangles represented by these crosses.
What is special about these rectangles?"

3. Square Numbers

Some children have imagined that the yellow cross is where two yellow cars crash head on!
Explain to children that numbers represented by these crosses are called square numbers.
The shape of the rectangle will make this obvious.
e.g.
"4 x 4 is a square number.
This is called 4 to the power of 2 or 4 'squared'.
"*How many square numbers can you find?*
Make these 'numbers' with the rods.
Is there any pattern in the way they are growing.
Do you notice a pattern about where they are found on the Colour Square?"

Children could colour their attempts on graph paper.

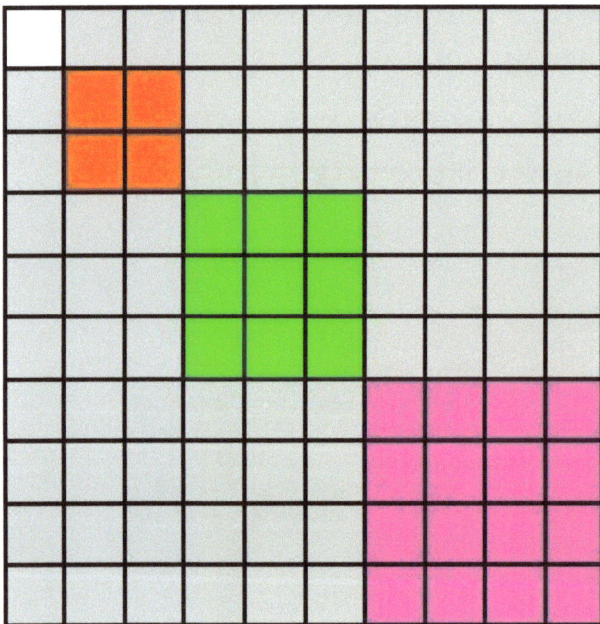
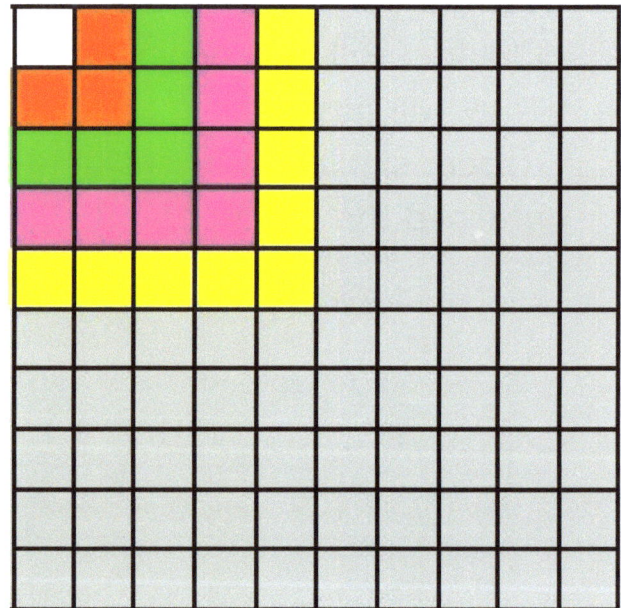

Fig 1   **Fig 2**

The power of colour suggests a pattern for growth,
Figure 1 is fairly obvious.
Figure 2 less so:

$$1 = 1 + 0$$
$$4 = 1 + 3$$
$$9 = 1 + 3 + 5 = (1 + 3) + 5 = 4 + 5$$
$$16 = 1 + 3 + 5 + 7 = ((1 + 3) + 5) + 7 = (4 + 5) + 7 = 9 + 7$$
$$25 = . . . \text{ etc}$$

Children may well make their own suggestions.
Another idea is to ask children to use the biggest square number they have made as the base and place the next biggest square on top until they end up with something like Fig 2.

4. Division.

Division can be shown to be the inverse of multiplication quite easily using the square.

e.g.

   5 x 3 = 15 therefore 15 ÷ 5 = 3 or 15 ÷ 3 = 5

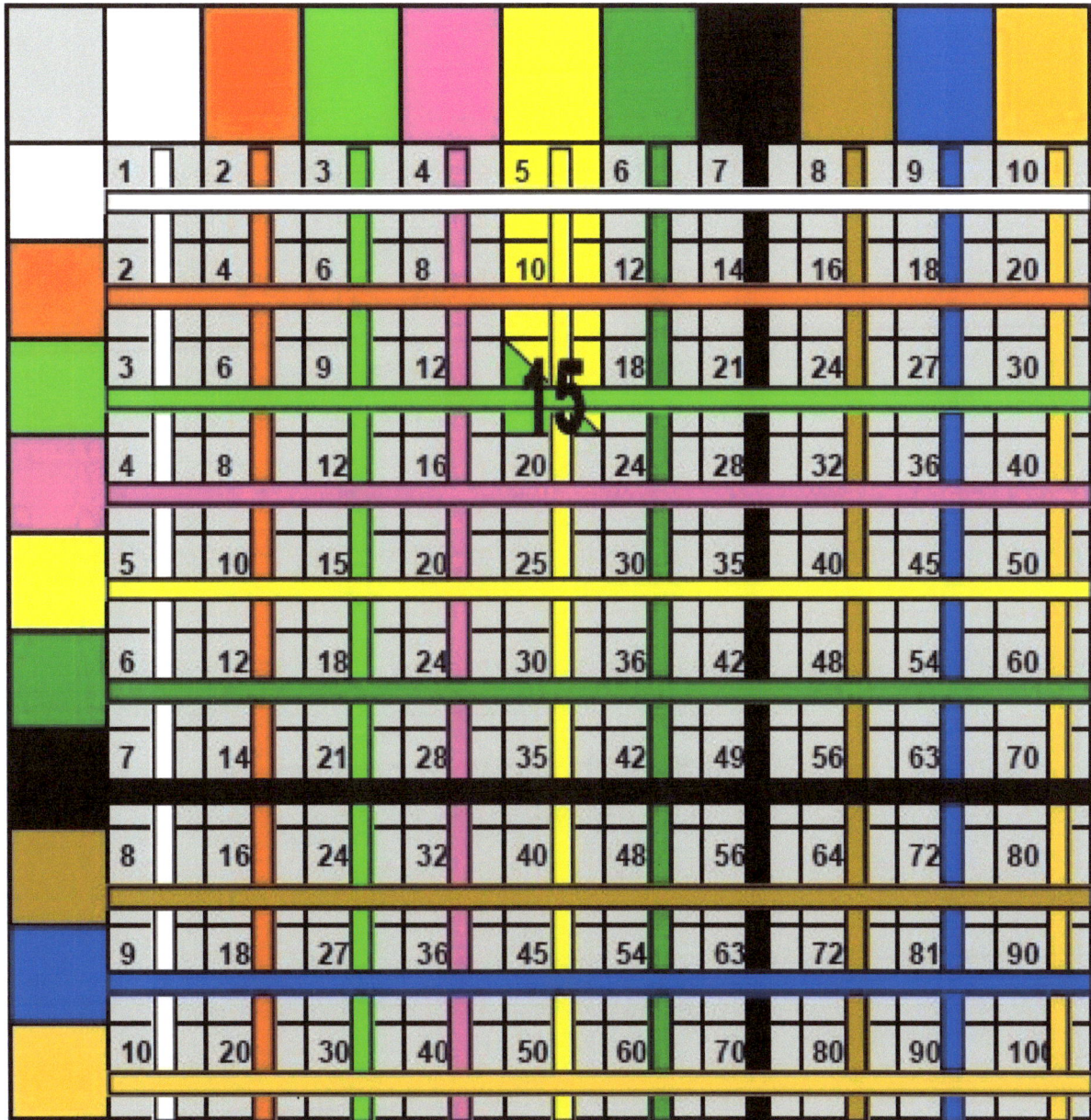

To find 15 ÷ 5 you would say:

"*Move down the yellow column/ path/ street . . .*
until you reach 15. Which rod makes the cross with yellow?"

The answer is light green or 3.

This can be represented with the rods as:

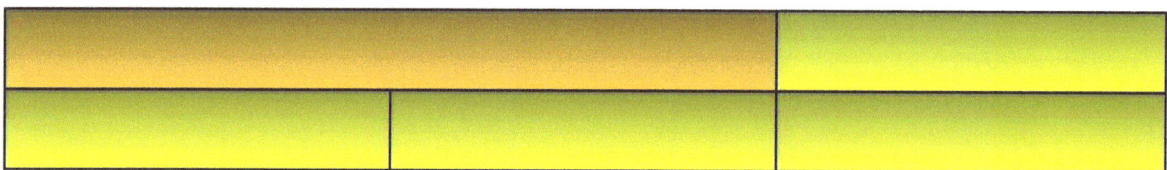

Try this with 15 ÷ 5

Give lots of examples until you are sure children have grasped the concept.

e.g. 24 ÷ 6 36 ÷ 9 48 ÷ 8 etc . . .

To consolidate children's understanding you could ask, "*What colour path would I need to follow to find the answer to:*

35 ÷ 5   27 ÷ 9   64 ÷ 8   28 ÷ 7 . . . etc?"

They need only give the colour names of the rods or hold the rods up in response.

You can now be sure they are giving the rods the correct number names and that they understand division, like multiplication has to do with 'whole groups' of numbers.

5. Division With Remainders

Once children understand how to use the Amazing Colour Factor Multiplication Square for multiplication and division
the concept of remainders is easily introduced.
Ask the child to,

"Divide 24 by 5"

Children will immediately realise they have to follow the yellow pattern/column.

This time however 24 cannot be found.

Ask,

"What number is nearest 24?"

One child might suggest 20, another 25.

"As they are both 'next door' to each other which should we choose?"

Hopefully someone will suggest 20 because although 25 is only 1 away from 24 it is too big.

We always choose the next smallest number.

Using the rods the pattern would look like this:

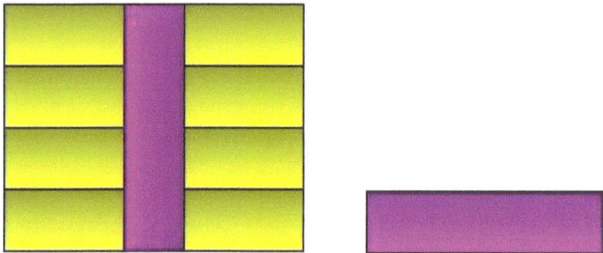

24 ÷ 5 = 4 remainder 4 or 24 = (4 x 5) + 4

Give plenty of examples until children are confident.

6. Fractions As Operators

This a natural progression from division.

Method 1:

Ask: "*What is 16 ÷ 2?*"

Children will use the Colour Factor Multiplication Square or visualise the answer in their head.

Fig 1

Because red (2) is 8 times smaller than orange plus dark green (16)

We can say it is "*one eight of sixteen*".

1/8 x 16 is simply another way of saying 16 ÷ 2.

  1/3 x 9   1/5 x 10   1/7 x 28 . . . etc?

By following the tan line children can immediately 'see' which numbers are 1/8 of another number just by looking at the 'crosses'.

White (1) is 1/8 of 8

Red (2) is 1/8 of 16

Light green (3) is 1/8 of 24 etc

Try this with other colour lines e.g. dark green (6)

This time they will be finding 1/6 of the number in the squares.

e.g.

White is 1/6 of 6

Red is 1/6 of 12 . . .

Method 2.

Now try asking:

"*What is one sixth of eighteen.*"

"*Make the train equivalent to 18.*

Now make a train of one colour equal to orange and tan (18) but you can only use six rods."

Some children will 'see' it straight away. Others will enjoy solving the 'jigsaw'.

Alternate these two methods using varied examples until the concept of fractions as operators is fully grasped.

7. Introducing Numerators

It is now a small step to extend the work with fractions further.

Children discovered that fractions as operators act in the same way as division.

eg 1/4 x 24 is the same as 24 ÷ 4

It is simply a different way of expressing the same function.

In each case the colour path we followed was determined by either the divisor or the denominator.

e.g. 1/**4** x 24 or 24 ÷ **4**

Now throw down the challenge to find 3/4 x 24

Once again it is the denominator that determines down which colour path we travel.

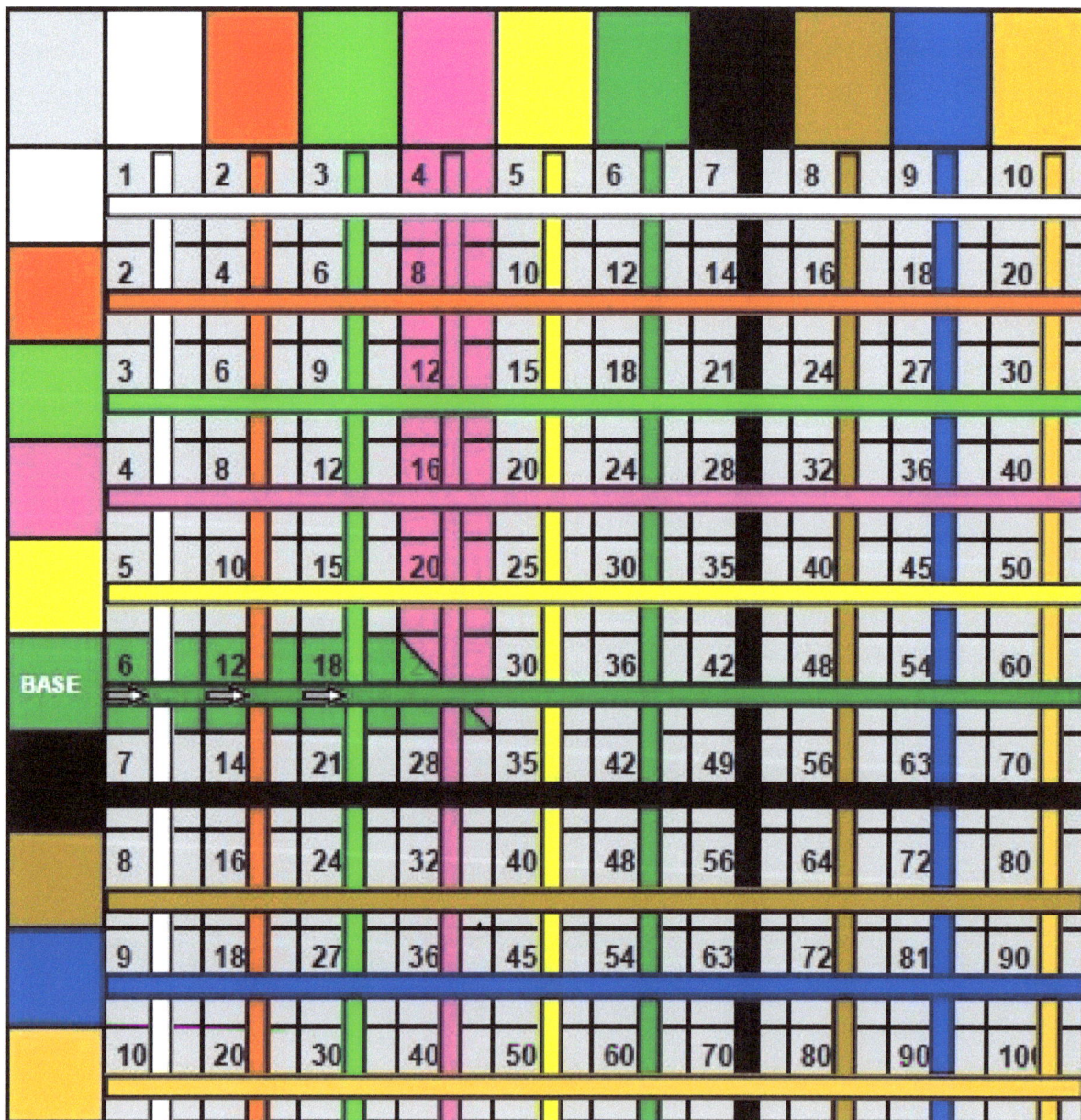

e.g. 3/**4** x 24

"*Follow the pink path till you reach 24.*

What colour path crosses the pink path? (dark green)

Follow the dark green path back to its base.
(Plenty of scope for the imagination here).

*Now what is the number on the top of the fraction,
the numerator? (3)*

Follow the dark green path back three squares.

What number do you end up on?
(18)

Provide lots of example orally to begin with:
e.g. 3/4 x 20   3/8 x 24   4/5 x 20   2/7 x 21   4/6 x 18   5/9 x 45
    5/4 x 36 . . . etc.
Use the rods to help visualise the process for children having difficulty.
eg 3/4 x 24

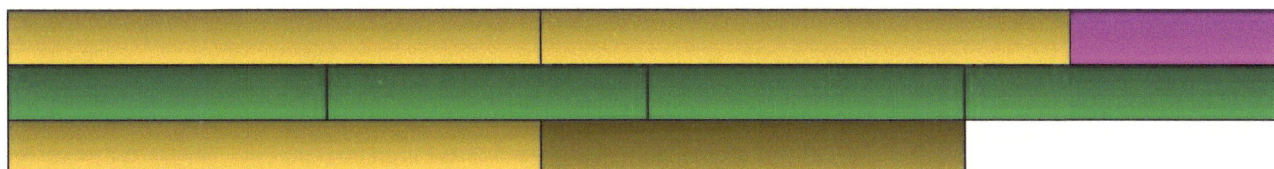

8. Factors
Ask children to make a train equivalent to 24.

Now say:
"Make as many trains as possible of one colour equal to 24".

The numbers represented by each colour are said to be 'factors' of 24. This could be represented as a map.

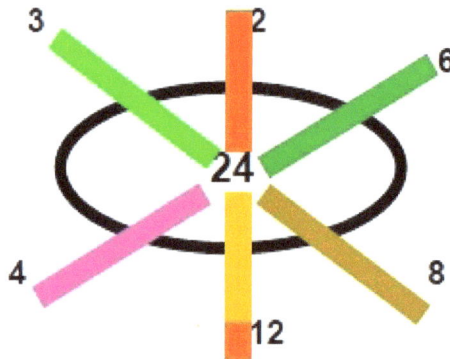

Use the 'factor table' for 24 to reinforce concepts already covered.
e.g.
Look at the table. Which rod is equivalent to:

1/3 x 24   1/4 x 24   1/6 x 24   1/12 x 24 . . . etc

Which rod is equivalent to:

2/3 x 24   3/4 x 24   7/8 x 24   5/12 x 24 . . . etc

We could also write the pattern as multiplication or division:

4 x6 = 24   24 ÷ 6 = 4   6 x 4 = 24   24 ÷ 4 = 6

Ask children to make a 'factor table' and a 'map' for 18, 36, 27 . . . etc

Again, provide many examples until the concept is grasped.

Another method of finding factors is to use the Amazing Colour Factor Multiplication Square.
Give a number, say 40, and ask children to find how many times 40 appears on the square.
They will find it appears four times.

Two pairs of squares are very similar.
The crosses are comprised of the same colours but children will know that they represent different 'rectangles'.
They are a visual reminder that multiplication is commutative.

4 x 10 = 10 x 4 = 8 x 5 = 5 x 8

Ask children how many different colors there are.
These colours represent the factors of 40.

i.e. 4, 10, 8, 5

Give many examples until children are confident in their ability to find factors.

The Amazing Colour Factor Multiplication Square

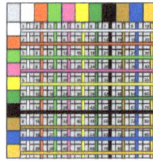

9. Prime Numbers

Once children have made numerous 'factor tables' they will notice that white appears in every one.

Some children may be able to tell you why.

Explain that some numbers only have two factors, white and themselves!.
These numbers will appear twice on the multiplication square.
They are called prime numbers.

Ask children which column they will always appear in.

Ask children to find as many 'prime number squares' as they can. e.g.

Why will they not find many?

Once again lots of examples should be given orally and the whole emphasis should be on the game.

Make it fun!

Ask children to find prime numbers on a 100 square.
Will they find more than they did on the multiplication square?

10. Fractions

Once again ask children to create a 'factor table' for 24.

"What fraction of 24 is 1?"

Remind children of the work you did with fractions as operators and the link with division.
White (1) is 24 times smaller than two orange plus red (24)
We call it 1/24."

"What fraction of 24 is 2 . . . 3 . . . 6 . . . 8 . . . 12?"
Hold up the different rods until children are instantly able to 'name' its relation to 24.

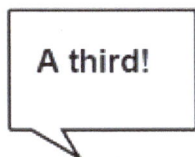

Having established 'fraction names' for the rods:
e.g. white (1/24); red (1/12); light green (1/8); dark green (1/4); tan (1/3; orange plus red (1/2) ;

Ask questions like:
"How many 1/4's (dark greens) equal 1/2 (orange plus red)?"
i.e. 1/2 = 2/4

Ask lots of questions until children answer almost instantly.
Now increase the challenge.

Ask questions like:
"How many 1/6's are there in 2/3?"
"How many 1/8's are equal to 3/4 . . . etc?"

Ask children to make 'factor tables' for different numbers and repeat the process.
Children will see that regardless of what 'table' is used relationships remain constant.
1/3 will always be equivalent to 2/6 no matter which rods represent one third or one sixth.
For example, if the 'factor table' is 12 then red will equal 1/6 and pink will equal 1/3.

 This kind of exercise gives children mental flexibility and encourages abstract thought.
(Our math program '**Child's Play Maths**', shows how by the age of six or seven children can have a thorough understanding of fractions).

11. Handling Data and Area

'Mental flexibility' is vital to continued successful mathematical development.
Although for most of the time we use the rods children will assume white represents 1, red 2, and so on.

They should never believe that white is 1, or red is 2 etc.

The rods can be used to introduce data handling with block graphs.
Children will be at a distinct disadvantage if they believe the rods have a fixed value.
e.g

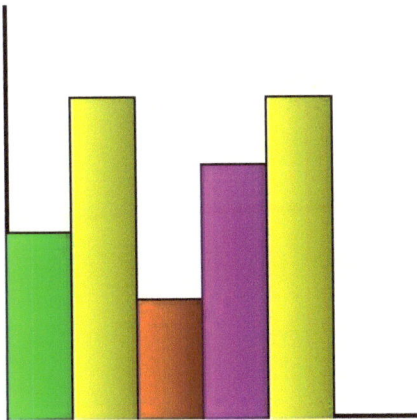

This could be a graph showing students who stayed up after 9 a.m. weekdays.
If it was a class project white would probably represent 1.
If it was a school project however, white would equal 10 or more.

The concept of averages can also be introduced graphically with the rods.

First we rearrange the graph into a train.
Then we ask how many rods the train is comprised of (five).
Now ask children to make a train equal to the one they have just made but they can only use rods of one colour and they are restricted to just five.

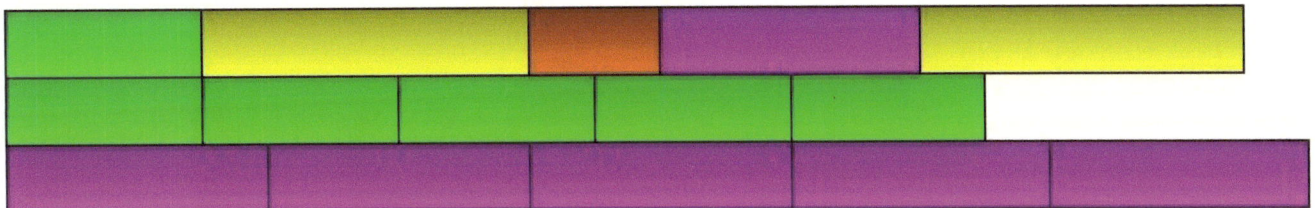

Children can see that the purple train is the closest.
The average is then seen to be, more than green (3) and slightly less than pink (4).

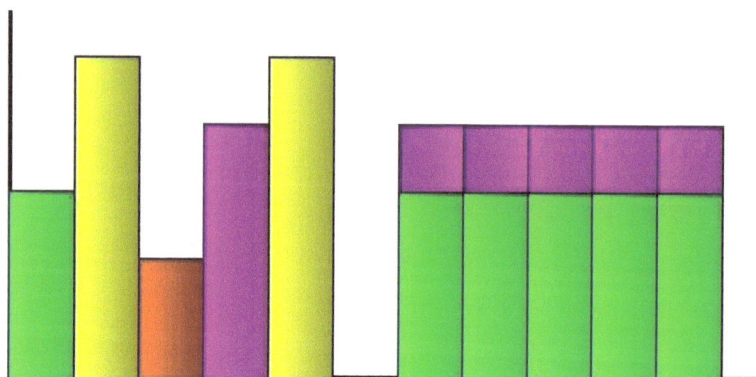

Having been introduced to the concept of fractions children will understand there are numbers that exist between whole numbers.
This is ideal preparation for the introduction of decimals.

Using the Colour Factor Multiplication Square children will be given an effective grounding for the introduction of area
and will have no problems with irregular shapes.
They will 'see' more than one possible solution.
Challenge students to find as many solutions as possible.

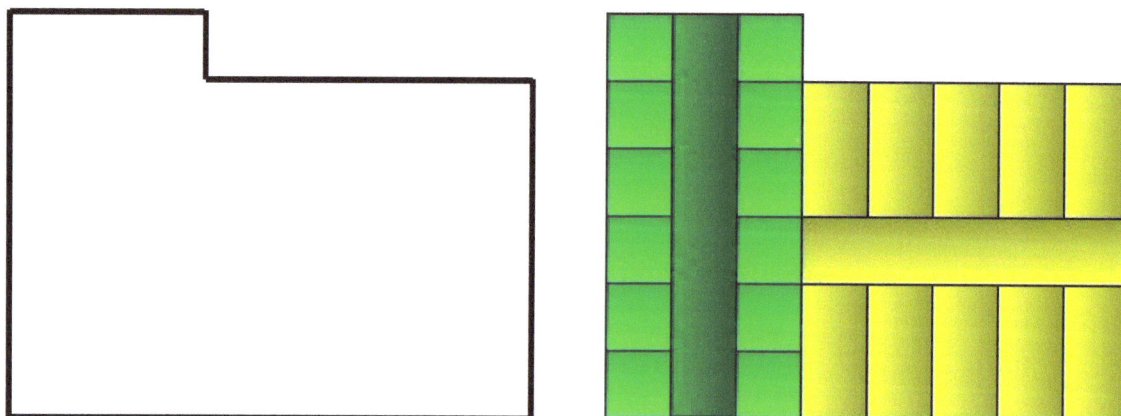

12. Pythagoras' Theorem

The ability to visualise is vital to our success in every area of life.

Using the rods will help your child cultivate the ability to mentally visualise what he/she is trying to express mathematically.
This is wonderful training for life itself.

I first understood Pythagoras' Theorem when I was able to visualise it using the rods.

Try it with your children.

Ask them to think of numbers that make a square, 'square numbers'.
They will remember that these numbers show up as a cross of one colour on the square.
e.g 1, 4, 9, 16, 25, 36 . . .

  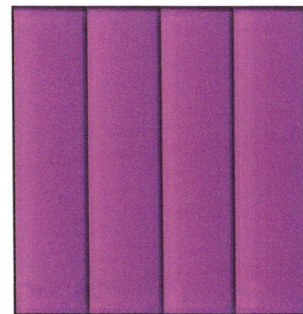

"Choose two 'square numbers' that added together equal a third."
e.g 9 + 16 = 25

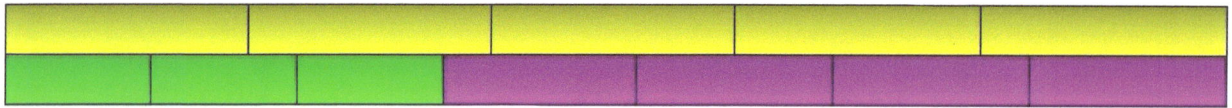

Children can make the two trains, yellow (five rods) and pink (four rods) plus green (five rods) and place them side by side to prove they are equal

"Make the 'square' for each number.

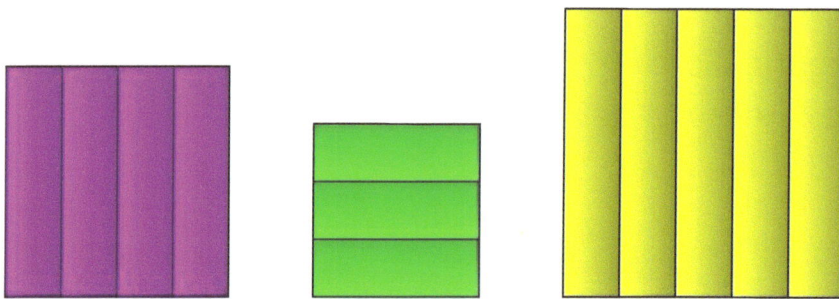

Join the edges of the squares."

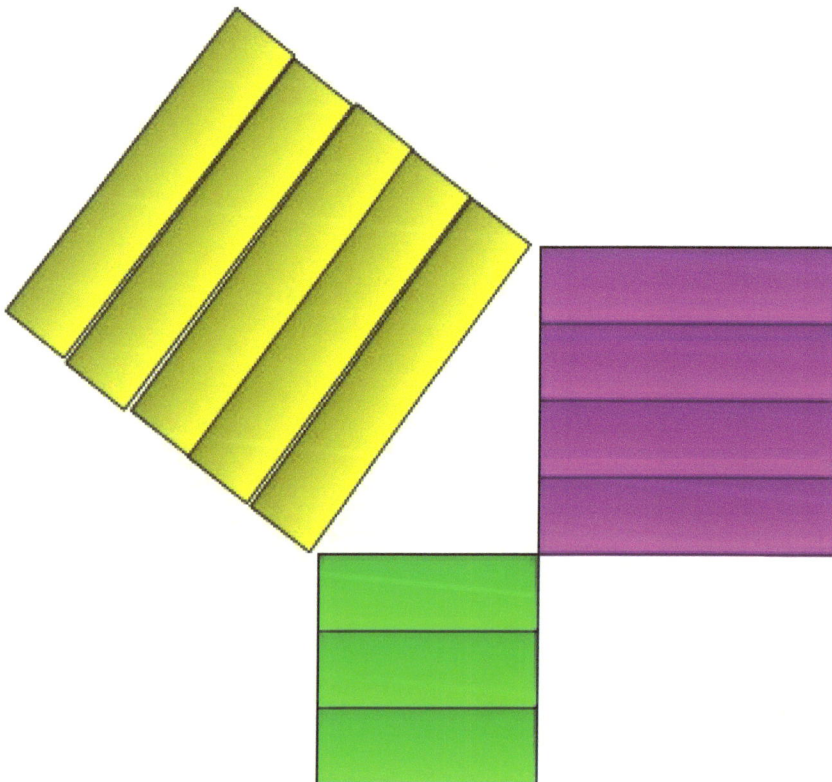

They make a triangle, a right-angled triangle.

The longest side is yellow.

This is called the hypotenuse.

The square it makes is equal to the sum of the other two squares added together.

$5y = 3g + 4p$

$5 \times 5 = (3 \times 3) + (4 \times 4)$

$25 = 9 + 16$

The Amazing Colour Factor Multiplication Square

	1	2	3	4	5	6	7	8	9	10
1	1	2	3	4	5	6	7	8	9	10
2	2	4	6	8	10	12	14	16	18	20
3	3	6	9	12	15	18	21	24	27	30
4	4	8	12	16	20	24	28	32	36	40
5	5	10	15	20	25	30	35	40	45	50
6	6	12	18	24	30	36	42	48	54	60
7	7	14	21	28	35	42	49	56	63	70
8	8	16	24	32	40	48	56	64	72	80
9	9	18	27	36	45	54	63	72	81	90
10	10	20	30	40	50	60	70	80	90	100

The Amazing Colour Factor Multiplication Square

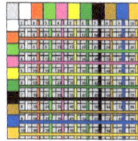

The square can be photocopied and laminated as many times as necessary to provide every child with their own copy.

This program builds on our introductory early years math program 'Child's Play Maths'.

For a free copy of our Cuisenaire Rods software app (Windows only) visit: www.helpyourchildsucceed.com/five.htm

Here are what teachers have said about the **software** and **Child's Play Maths**:

COMMENTS & RATINGS

On February 26, 2015, Ivonne Elizabeth C. said:

WOW!!!!!

Total:	⭐⭐⭐⭐ 4.0
Overall Quality:	⭐⭐⭐⭐ 4.0
Accuracy:	⭐⭐⭐⭐ 4.0
Practicality:	⭐⭐⭐⭐ 4.0
Thoroughness:	⭐⭐⭐⭐ 4.0
Creativity:	⭐⭐⭐⭐ 4.0
Clarity:	⭐⭐⭐⭐ 4.0

On July 23, 2014, By the Inch (TpT Seller) said:

Wow, thank you so much!

Total:	⭐⭐⭐⭐ 4.0
Overall Quality:	⭐⭐⭐⭐ 4.0
Accuracy:	⭐⭐⭐⭐ 4.0
Practicality:	⭐⭐⭐⭐ 4.0
Thoroughness:	⭐⭐⭐⭐ 4.0
Creativity:	⭐⭐⭐⭐ 4.0
Clarity:	⭐⭐⭐⭐ 4.0

On December 31, 2013, Deborah T. said:

Love it thank you. Can't wait to use it!

Total:	★★★★ 4.0
Overall Quality:	★★★★ 4.0
Accuracy:	★★★★ 4.0
Practicality:	★★★★ 4.0
Thoroughness:	★★★★ 4.0
Creativity:	★★★★ 4.0
Clarity:	★★★★ 4.0

On May 26, 2012, Teacher Kirra (TpT Seller) said:

Thank you! I can see so many uses for this.

Total:	★★★★ 4.0
Overall Quality:	★★★★ 4.0
Accuracy:	★★★★ 4.0
Practicality:	★★★★ 4.0
Thoroughness:	★★★★ 4.0
Creativity:	★★★★ 4.0
Clarity:	★★★★ 4.0

On May 14, 2013, Buyer said:

Thanks I needed a resource for Cuisenaire rods!

Total:	★★★★ N/A
Overall Quality:	★★★★ N/A
Accuracy:	★★★★ N/A
Practicality:	★★★★ N/A
Thoroughness:	★★★★ N/A
Creativity:	★★★★ N/A
Clarity:	★★★★ N/A

On May 12, 2014, Eugenia B. said:

I love this approach to teaching math with my special needs students. I've been using the rods for awhile now and it was great to see the "rod" math broken down into units. I was disappointed in the attached u tube videos embedded in the document. They are quite short and the final image goes away after it plays.--I wouldn't be able to use it on my smart board.

Total:	★★★★ 3.7
Overall Quality:	★★★★ 4.0
Accuracy:	★★★★ 4.0
Practicality:	★★★★ 3.0
Thoroughness:	★★★★ 3.0
Creativity:	★★★★ 4.0
Clarity:	★★★★ 4.0

On November 19, 2014, Joanne G. said:

Great resource. thank you!

Total:	★★★★ 4.0
Overall Quality:	★★★★ 4.0
Accuracy:	★★★★ 4.0
Practicality:	★★★★ 4.0
Thoroughness:	★★★★ 4.0
Creativity:	★★★★ 4.0
Clarity:	★★★★ 4.0

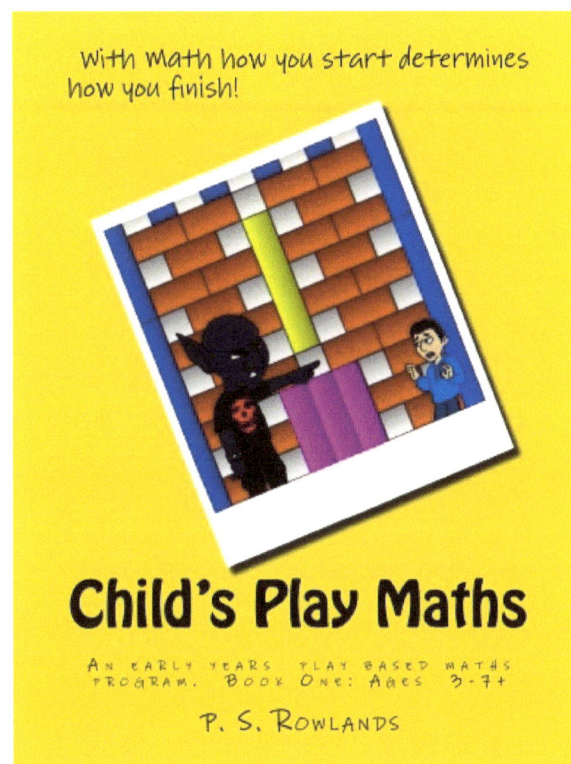

With Math how you start determines how you finish!

Child's Play Maths

AN EARLY YEARS PLAY BASED MATHS PROGRAM. BOOK ONE: AGES 3-7+

P. S. ROWLANDS

Child's Play Maths 2 is now available from Amazon.

www.ingramcontent.com/pod-product-compliance
Lightning Source LLC
Chambersburg PA
CBHW041550040426
42447CB00002B/119